Julius Waterbury

Choral praise

Songs and anthems, for Sunday schools and choral societies

Julius Waterbury

Choral praise
Songs and anthems, for Sunday schools and choral societies

ISBN/EAN: 9783337266400

Printed in Europe, USA, Canada, Australia, Japan

Cover: Foto ©Thomas Meinert / pixelio.de

More available books at **www.hansebooks.com**

CHORAL PRAISE:

SONGS AND ANTHEMS,

FOR

SUNDAY SCHOOLS

AND

CHORAL SOCIETIES.

BY THE

Rev. JULIUS HENRY WATERBURY, A.M.

AUTHOR OF "COMMON PRAISE."

Al - le - lu - ia.

Praise ye the Lord.

BOSTON:

PUBLISHED BY OLIVER DITSON & COMPANY,

NEW YORK: PHILADELPHIA: CHICAGO:
C. H. DITSON & Co.   J. E. DITSON & Co.   LYON & HEALY.

Entered according to Act of Congress, in the year 1871,
By J. H. WATERBURY,
In the Office of the Librarian of Congress, at Washington.

A Service for Choirs and Congregations

AT THE

REHEARSALS OF CHURCH MUSIC.

Let the peo - ple praise Thee, O God;

Yea, let all..... the peo - ple praise Thee.

Chant the Psalm, with Gloria Patri.

The Lord be with you.
R. And with Thy Spirit.

Let us pray.

O Lord, show Thy mercy upon us.
R. And grant us Thy salvation.
V. O God, make clean our hearts within us.
R. And take not Thy Holy Spirit from us.

GRANT, O Lord, that what we shall say or sing with our mouth we may believe in our hearts; and that what we believe in our hearts we may fulfill in our lives, through Jesus Christ our Lord. *Amen.*

ACCEPT, O Lord, we beseech Thee, the hearty endeavors of us Thy humble servants to praise Thy Holy Name, and grant that the work wherein we are engaged may by Thy grace be made effectual to the advancement of our souls in Thy Faith, Fear, and Love, through Jesus Christ our Lord. *Amen.*

Benediction.

The grace of our Lord, &c.

The Elements of Vocal Music.

LESSON I.

THE SCALE comprises eight tones with seven intervals, consisting of five *Major* and two *Minor Seconds*.

1	2	3	4	5	6	7	8
Do	Re	Mi	Fa	Sol	La	Si	Do.
C	D	E	F	G	A	B	C.

Now we sing through the upward scale,
Now we sing through the downward scale.

Hymn 1. L. M.

Praise God, from whom all blessings flow;
Praise Him, all creatures here below;
Praise Him above, angelic Host,
Praise Father, Son, and Holy Ghost.

Hymn 2. L. M.

Speak gently to the little child,
Teach it in accents soft and mild;
Speak gently, kindly, to the poor,
They have enough they must endure.

Hymn 3. 8s & 7s.

1 In the pleasant, sunny meadows,
  Where the buttercups are seen;
And the daisies' little shadows
  Lie along the level green:

2 Flocks of quiet sheep are feeding,
  Little lambs are playing near;
For the watchful shepherd leading,
  Keeps them safe from harm and fear.

3 Christians are like sheep, abiding
  In the Church's pasture free;
Jesus is our Shepherd guiding,
  And the little lambs are we.

4 O sweet Shepherd, gently lead us,
  Lest we fall or go astray;
With the Bread of Heaven O feed us,
  That we faint not by the way.

LESSON II.

THE STAFF consists of five lines and four spaces, with lines above and below. The *Clefs* determine the letters on the degrees of the staff. *Bars* and *Measures* are rhythmic marks.

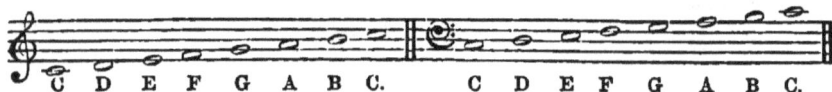

4. The Lord my pasture shall prepare,
And feed me with a shepherd's care.

5. Round.

1   3 | 5   5 | 3   5 | 8 || 8   5 | 8   8 · 8 | 5   5 | 3

Morn - ing bells I love to hear, Ring-ing mer-ri - ly, loud and clear.

6. Chant.   5 | 6   5 | 8 || 7 | 8   6 | 5   4 | 8

Glory be to the Father, | and · to the | Son, || and | to the | Holy | Ghost;
As it was in the beginning, is now, and | ever · shall | be || world | without | end. A- |
men.

Hymn 7.   8s & 7s.

1 Heavenly Father, | send thy | blessing
    On thy | children | gathered | here,
May they all, thy | name con- | fessing,
    Be to | Thee for- | ever | dear ;
May they be, like | Joseph, | loving,
    Duti- | ful and | chaste and | pure ;
And their faith like | David | proving,
    Steadfast | unto | death en- | dure.

2 Holy Saviour, | who in | meekness
    Didst vouch- | safe a | Child to | be,
Guide their steps, and | help their | weakness,
    Bless and | make them | like to | Thee ;
Bear Thy lambs when | they are | weary
    In Thine | arms, and | at Thy | breast ;
Through life's desert, | dry and | dreary,
    Bring them | to thy | heavenly | rest.

3 Spread Thy golden | pinions | o'er them,
    Holy | Spirit, | Heavenly | Dove,
Guide them, lead them, | go be- | fore them,
    Give them | peace, and | joy, and | love ;
Temples of the | Holy | Spirit
    May they | with Thy | glory | shine,
And immortal | bliss in- | herit
    And for | ever- | more be | thine ! Amen.

LESSON III.

Notes and Marks of Silence.

8. Round.

Let us then be up and do - ing With a heart for a - ny fate;
Still a - chiev-ing, still pur - su - ing, Learn to la - bor and to wait.

9. Round for Three Voices.

The sun is sink-ing, Let us try sing-ing, To close our eve - ning.

10. LITTLE DROPS OF WATER.

Lit - tle drops of wa - ter, Lit - tle grains of sand,..

Make the might-y o - cean And the beau-teous land...

2 And the little moments,
  Humble though they be,
Make the mighty ages
  Of Eternity.

3 So our little errors
  Lead the soul away
From the path of virtue
  Oft in sin to stray.

4 Little deeds of kindness,
  Little words of love,
Make our earth an Eden
  Like the heaven above.

LESSON IV.

The Chromatic Scale, and the Transposition of the Major Scale.

♯ = *Sharp.*   ♭ = *Flat.*   ♮ = *Natural.*

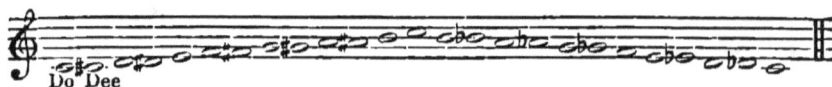

Do Dee

Key of G—Signature, one Sharp.

C D E F G A B C   Do   Do

11. THE SPRING IS COME. Round for Three Voices.

The spring is come, I hear the birds, That sing from bush to bush;

Hark! hark! I hear them sing:

The lin - net and the lit - tle wren, The black-bird and the thrush.

12. SWEETLY NOW THE BELLS. Round.

Sweet - ly now the bells are ring - ing, Call to church for

prayer and sing - ing. Ding dong, ding dong.

13. CHEERILY, CHEERILY. Round for Three Voices.

Cheer - i - ly, cheer - i - ly sound the strain, Hap - pi - ly, hap - pi - ly

met a - gain; All, all, all are here.

14. BRIGHTLY GLEAMS OUR BANNER.

From HAYDN. *Arranged by* Rev. J. B. DYKES.

1. Brightly gleams our ban-ner, Point-ing to the sky, Wav-ing wanderers

on - ward To their home on high. Journeying o'er a des - ert,

Glad - ly thus we pray, And, with hearts u - nit - ed, Take our heavenward

Chorus.

way..... Bright-ly gleams our ban - ner,.. Point-ing to the sky,

Wav-ing wan-derers on - ward To their home on high. A - men.

2 Hail! sweet Jesus, Master,
    Round Thy Sacred Feet,
    Here, with hearts rejoicing,
      See Thy children meet.
Long, alas! we've left Thee
    Straying far away,
Now once more we'll enter
    On the narrow way.
Cho.—Brightly gleams our banner, &c.

3 All our days direct us,—
    Make us meek and mild,
By Thy Childhood's Pattern,—
    Mary's Holy Child.
Bid Thine angels shield us,
    When the storm-clouds lower,

Pardon Thou—protect us
    At death's solemn hour.
Cho.—Brightly gleams our banner, &c.

4 Jesu! Saints and Angels
    With Thy Church combine,
Offering prayers and praises
    At Thy glorious shrine;
When the toil is over,
    Then comes rest and peace,
Jesus in His beauty,—
    Songs that never cease,
Cho.—Brightly gleams our banner,
    Pointing to the sky,
Waving wanderers onward
    To their home on high.   Amen.

Key of D—Signature, two Sharps.

C D E F G A B C.   Do   Do

15. JESUS, HOLY, UNDEFILED.

1. Je - sus, ho - ly, un - de - filed, List-en   to   a   lit - tle child;

Thou hast sent the glo-rious light Chasing far the si - lent night. *A - men.*

2 Thou hast sent the sun to shine
    O'er this glorious world of Thine;
Warmth to give, and pleasant glow,
    On each tender flower below.

3 Thou by whom the birds are fed,
    Give to me my daily bread;

And Thy Holy Spirit give,
    Without whom I cannot live.

4 Make me, Lord, obedient, mild,
    As becomes a little child;
All day long, in every way,
    Teach me what to do and say.

16. A PARISH SCHOOL ROUND.

Words by J. H. W.

O cheer-i - ly, mer-ri- ly sing the song That tells of joy and gladness, As

Hur-rah! hurrah! hur-rah!..... The tones of the music implores us To be

Hark! hark! forward! 'Tis the bell, 'tis the parish school bell.

hap-pi- ly, hopeful-ly, thus we strive To o - vercome thoughts of sad - ness.

hap - py, truthful, and pure, As we aim for the joys be - fore us.

Hark! hark! forward! 'Tis the bell, 'tis the parish school bell...

Key of A—Signature, three Sharps.

C D E F G A B C. Do Do

17. GOD'S CARE.

1. When we in the mid-night sleep, Guardian an - gels watch do keep,
2. Hear our cheer-ful, heart- felt praise For Thy good- ness and Thy care;

When in slum - ber we are blest, God still watch-es o'er our rest.
May we be, thro' all our days, Safe - ly kept from ev - ery snare.

18. HAIL, HAPPY MORNING.

By permission from "THE PRIZE."

1. Hail, hap - py morn-ing! hail, ho - ly day! Call - ing from earth-ly

la - bors a - way; Sweet words of wis - dom, glad songs of joy,
"Come to the tem - ple, come, come a - way,

Fine.   Chorus.

Now be our best em - ploy. Sing once more the hap - py,
Hal - low the Lord's own day."

D. C.

hap - py song, While the gold - en mo - ments roll a - long:

2 Emblem of heaven, sweet day of rest,
In thy "remembrance" may we be blest;
So may our songs and lives ever say,
"Hallow the Lord's own day."—*Cho.*

3 Rest from our labors, rest from our cares;
Rest in our praises, rest in our prayers;
So the commandment would we obey:
"Hallow the Lord's own day."—*Cho.*

Key of E—Signature, four Sharps.

C D E F G A B C. Do   Do

19. SWEET HOME.

BISHOP.

1. 'Mid pleas - ures and pal - a - ces though we may roam, Be it
2. An ex - ile from home, pleasure daz - zles in vain, Oh,...

ev - er so hum - ble, there's no place like home! A charm
give me my low - ly - thatched cot - tage a - gain The birds

from the skies seem to hal - low us there, Which, seek thro' the
sing - ing gai - ly, that came at my call, Give me them, with the

world, is not met with else - where. Home, home, sweet, sweet
peace of mind dear - er than all. Home, home, &c.

home, There's no place like home, There's no place like home.

20. MORNING THOUGHTS.

1. O blessed Sav- iour, Lord a - bove, So lov - ing and so mild,
2. Let ev - ery thought with-in my mind Be pure and free from sin,
3. I know that Thou wilt hear a child, A lit - tle child like me:

Look down up - on me thro' this day, Bless me, a lit - tle child.
And may my words show all a - round That Thou dost rule with - in.
And help me to be kind and true, As ev - ery child should be.

21. GOOD NIGHT SONG.

1. Now the qui - et shades are fall - ing Soft- ly round each low - ly dwelling;
2. Ho - ly an - gels round us bend-ing, Peace on love's bright wings descending;
3. Hand in hand our path pur - su - ing, Day by day our joys re - new- ing;

Sweet our eve-ning hymn is swelling, Schoolmates dear, good night, good night.
With our eve-ning wor - ship blending, Schoolmates, &c.
Here our words and deeds re - view-ing, Schoolmates, &c.

Key of F—Signature, one Flat.

C D E F G A B C Do   Do

22. FROM THE HEAVENS ABOVE.

1. From the heavens a - bove Our God, in mer - cy mild,
2. Hears his ev - ery prayer, Is faith - ful day and night,

With a Fa - ther's love, Looks down on.. ev - ery child:
With a Fa - ther's care Sur - rounds his steps with light.

23. Round for Three Voices.

Be you to oth - ers kind and true, And al - ways un - to

oth - ers do As you'd have oth - ers do to you.

24. BRIGHTEST AND BEST.

Alto Solo.   Chorus.   MENDELSSOHN.

1. Bright-est and best of the sons of the morn-ing, Dawn on our
2. Low on His cra - dle the dew - drops are shin - ing, Low lies His

Soprano Solo.

dark-ness, and lend us thine aid: Star of the east, the ho - ri -
head with the beasts of the stall; An - gels a - dore Him in slum-

Chorus.

zon a - dorn - ing, Guide where our In - fant Re - deem - er is laid.
ber re - clin - ing, Mak - er and Mon - arch, and Sav - iour of all.

Key of B♭—Signature, two Flats.

C D E F G A B C.   Do   Do

25. COME, FOLLOW ME. Round.

Come,   fol - low, fol - low, fol - low, fol - low, fol - low, fol - low me.
Come,   ev - ery son and daughter, Join the prais-es we would sing;

Whither shall I fol-low, fol - low, fol - low, Whither shall I follow, fol-low thee?
For it is a pleasure cheering, bet - ter Far than anything that we can bring.

Down by the willow, wil - low, wil-low, Down by the wil - low, wil - low tree,
Prais - es to Him, the Sav-iour, Brother, Prais - es to Him, the Might-y King.

26. PRAISE.

Arr. from HAYDN.

1. O heavenly Fa - ther, bow Thine ear, And heark-en to Thy

serv - ants here, While we our youth-ful voi - ces raise In fer - vent

prayers.. and songs...... of praise. Glad - ly to..... Thy

In fer-vent prayers and songs of praise.

Chorus.

courts we come, O guide.. us to...... our heaven-ly home.

2 From out the busy ways of life,
  From all its pleasures and its strife,
  We seek, O Lord, Thy loving face,
  And beg the treasures of Thy grace:
    Gladly to Thy courts we come,
    O guide us to our heavenly home.

3 Teach us, dear Lord, Thy way to know,
  And help us in that way to go,
  That so our walk with Thee begun

May in Thy footsteps always run:
  Gladly to Thy courts we come,
  O guide us to our heavenly home.

4 Let the sweet sunshine of Thy love,
  Still hovering o'er us like the dove,
  Fill all our hearts and homes with joy,
  And all our grateful hours employ:
    Gladly to Thy courts we come,
    O lead us to our heavenly home.

Key of E♭—Signature, three Flats.

C D E F G A B C. Do Do

27. WHEN THE MORN IS BRIGHT. BLUMENTHAL.

1. When the morn is bright and fair, When sweet songsters charm the air,

I will lift my heart in prayer, I will seek my Fa - ther;

Lest my feet should go a - stray From His pure and per - fect way;

Lest I grieve Him as I may, I will seek my Fa - ther.

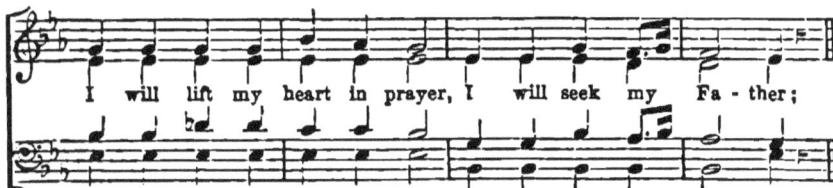

2 In the solitude apart,
　In the wilderness or mart,
　Oh! my sorely tempted heart,
　　I will seek my Father;
　In the darkness as the day,
　He shall be my Guide and Stay;
　I will lean on Him alway—
　　I will seek my Father.

3 When the evening sun is red,
　When each blossom droops its head,
　Kneeling low beside my bed,
　　I will seek my Father;
　That I slumber in His care,
　Shielded from each harmful snare;
　And for life or death prepare;
　　I will seek my Father.

Key of A♭—Signature, four Flats.

C D E F G A B C.   Do   Do

28. BE KIND TO THY FATHER.

1. Be kind to thy fa - ther—for when thou wert young, Who loved thee so

fond-ly as he? He caught the first accents that fell from thy tongue And

joined in thy in - no - cent glee. Be kind to thy fa - ther—for

now he is old, His locks in-ter-min-gled with gray, His footsteps are

fee - ble, once fear - less and bold; Thy fa - ther is pass - ing a - way.

2 Be kind to thy mother,—for, lo, on her brow,
   May traces of sorrow be seen;
Oh, well may'st thou cherish and comfort her now,
   For loving and kind hath she been.
Remember thy mother,—for thee will she pray
   As long as God giveth her breath:
With accents of kindness then cheer her lone way
   E'en to the dark valley of death.

8 Be kind to thy brother—his heart will have dearth
   If the smile of thy joy be withdrawn;
The flowers of feeling will fade at their birth
   If the dew of affection be gone.

Be kind to thy brother—wherever you are
The love of a brother shall be
An ornament purer and richer by far
Than pearls from the depth of the sea.

4 Be kind to thy sister—not many may know
The depth of true sisterly love;
The wealth of the ocean lies fathoms below
The surface that sparkles above.
Be kind to thy father—once fearless and bold;
Be kind to thy mother, so near;
Be kind to thy brother, nor show thy heart cold;
Be kind to thy sister so dear.

29. Round.

He who would lead a hap-py life, He who would lead a hap-py life, Must keep him-self from an-gry strife, from an - gry strife, from an-gry strife.

30. THE REAPER AND THE FLOWERS.

1 THERE is a Reaper whose name is Death,
 And with his | sickle | keen,
He reaps the bearded grain at a breath,
 And the | flowers that | grow be-| tween.

2 "Shall I have naught that is fair?" saith
 he;
 "Have naught but the|bearded|grain?
Tho' the breath of these flow'rs is sweet to
I'll give|them all|back a-|gain." [me,

3 He gazed at the flowers with tearful eyes,
 He kissed their | drooping | leaves;
It was for the Lord in Paradise
 He | bound them | in his | sheaves.

4 "My Lord has need of these flow'rets
 The Reaper | said, and | smil'd; [gay,"

"Dear tokens of the earth are they,
 Where | He was | once a | child.

5 "They shall all bloom in fields of light,
 Transplanted | by my | care,
And saints upon their garments white,
 These | sacred | blossoms | wear."

6 And the mother gave in tears and pain
 The flowers she | most did | love;
She knew she should find them all again
 In the | fields of | light a- | bove.

7 Oh, not in cruelty, not in wrath,
 The Reaper | came that | day;
'Twas an angel visited the green earth,
 And | took the | flow'rs a- | way.

31. MY MOTHER DEAR.

8. LOVER.

1. There was a place in child-hood, That I re-mem-ber well;

And there a voice, of sweet-est tone, Bright fair-y tales did tell;

And gen-tle words and fond em-brace Were given with joy to me,

When I was in that hap-py place, Up-on my moth-er's knee.

My moth-er dear, my moth-er dear, My gen-tle, gen-tle moth-er.

2 When fairy tales were ended,
 "Good night," she softly said,
And kissed, and laid me down to sleep,
 Within my tiny bed;
And holy words she taught me there;
 Methinks I yet can see
Her angel eye, as close I knelt
 Beside my mother's knee,
 My mother dear, my mother dear,
 My gentle, gentle mother.

3 In the sickness of my childhood,
 The perils of my prime,
The sorrows of my riper years,
 The cares of every time:
When doubt and danger weighed me down,
 Then pleading all for me,
It was a fervent prayer to heaven
 That bent my mother's knee.
 My mother dear, my mother dear,
 My gentle, gentle mother.

32. I LOVE THE CHURCH.

Words by Rt. Rev. A. C. Coxe, D.D.

1. I love the Church, the ho - ly Church, The Sav - iour's spot-less Bride;

And oh, I love her pal - a - ces, Thro' all the world so wide.

2 The cross-topped spire amid the trees
 The holy bell of prayer,
The music of our Mother's voice,—
 Our Mother's home is there.

3 Unbroken is her lineage,
 Her warrant clear as when
Thou, Saviour, didst go up on high,
 And give good gifts to men.

4 Here clothed in innocence they stand,
 Thine holy orders three,

To rule and feed Thy flock, O Christ,
 And ever watch for Thee.

5 I love the Church—the holy Church—
 That o'er our life presides—
The birth, the bridal, and the grave,
 And many an hour besides.

6 Be mine through life to live in her,
 And when the Lord shall call,
To die in her, the Spouse of Christ,
 The Mother of us all.

33. FRANK. L. M.

J. H. W.

1. How sweet the les-sons, how divine, Which in the life of Je - sus shine!

How bright the wis-dom and the grace, Which in each word and act had place!

2 He never sought Himself to please,
Nor live on earth a life of ease,
But ceaselessly did He pursue
The business which He came to do.

3 A little child, His spirit still
Moved sweetly to His Father's will;
The manger and the cross declare
How perfect His example there.

4 Oh, be that dear example mine!
In me, may His sweet Spirit shine!
In some small measure may I be
A faithful copy, Lord, of Thee!

34. Awake, my soul. L. M.

1 AWAKE, my soul, to grateful lays,
And sing Thy great Redeemer's praise:
He justly claims a song from Thee;
His loving-kindness, oh, how free!

2 He saw me ruined in the fall,
Yet loved me notwithstanding all;
He saved me from my lost estate;
His loving-kindness, oh, how great!

3 Though numerous hosts of mighty foes,
Though earth and hell my way oppose,

He safely leads my soul along;
His loving-kindness, oh, how strong!

4 When trouble like a gloomy cloud,
Has gathered thick and thundered loud,
He near my soul has always stood;
His loving-kindness, oh, how good!

35. Advent. L. M.

1 WHEN Christ came down on earth of old,
He took our nature, poor and low;
He wore no form of angel mould,
But shared our weakness and our woe:

2 But when He cometh back once more,
Then shall be set the great white throne;
And earth and heav'n shall flee before
The face of Him that sits thereon.

3 O Son of God! in glory crown'd,
The Judge ordain'd of quick and dead;
O Son of man! so pitying found
For all the tears thy people shed;

4 Be with us in that awful hour,
And by Thy crown, and by Thy grave,
And by Thy love and all Thy pow'r,
In that great Day of Judgment save!

36. Lent. L. M. *Tune*, p. 110, C. P.

1 How beauteous were the marks divine
That in Thy meekness used to shine!
That lit Thy lonely pathway, trod
In wondrous love, O Son of God!

2 Oh, who like Thee, so calm, so bright,
So pure, so made to live in light?
Oh, who like Thee did ever go
So patient through a world of woe?

8 Oh, who like Thee so humbly bore
The scorn, the scoffs of men, before?
So meek, forgiving, godlike, high,
So glorious in humility?

4 Oh, in Thy light be mine to go,
Illuming all my way of woe!
And give me ever on the road
To trace Thy footsteps, Son of God!

37. Morning. L. M.

1 New every morning is the love
Our wakening and uprising prove:
Thro' sleep and darkness safely brought,
Restored to life, and power, and thought.

2 New mercies, each returning day,
Hover around us while we pray:
New perils past, new sins forgiven,
New thoughts of God, new hopes of heaven.

3 If on our daily course our mind
Be set to hallow all we find,
New treasures still, of countless price,
God will provide for sacrifice.

4 The trivial round, the common task,
Will furnish all we need to ask,
Room to deny ourselves a road
To bring us daily nearer God.

38. Evening. L. M.

1 O Father, Who didst all things make
That heaven and earth might do Thy will,
Bless us this night for Jesu's sake,
And for Thy work preserve us still.

2 O Son, who didst redeem mankind,
And set the captive sinner free,
Keep us this night with peaceful mind,
That we may safe abide in Thee.

3 O Holy Ghost, Who by Thy power
The Church elect dost sanctify,
Seal us this night, and hour by hour
Our hearts and members purify.

4 To Father, Son, and Holy Ghost,
The God Whom heaven and earth adore,
From men and from the angel-host
Be praise and glory evermore.

39. Baptism. L. M.

1 Thy Cross, O Lord, the holy sign
That we, thereafter, should be Thine,
Was traced upon our infant brow,
And shall we fear to own it now?

2 O God, forbid: before the vain,
The proud, the scoffing, the profane,
We will, through grace, our Lord confess,
His faint but faithful witnesses.

3 His strength in weakness He displays,
From youthful lips He perfects praise,
And we, his little soldiers, stand
Strong in the might of His right hand.

4 Smile on us, Lord, and we will fear
Nor scorn, nor shame, whilst Thou art
near:
Reproach is glory, suffering rest,
If borne for Thee, if by Thee blest.

40. O Lord, behold. L. M.

1 O Lord, behold, before Thy throne,
A band of children lowly bend;
Thy face we seek, Thy name we own,
And pray that Thou wilt be our friend.

2 Thou didst on earth the young receive,
And gently fold them to Thy breast,
And say that such in heaven should live,
Forever safe, forever blest.

3 Thy Holy Spirit's aid impart,
That He may teach us how to pray;
Make us sincere, and let each heart
Delight to tread in wisdom's way.

4 Oh, let Thy grace our souls renew,
And seal a sense of pardon there:
Teach us Thy will to know and do,
And let us all Thine image bear.

41. KINGSLEY. C. M.

1. See the kind Shepherd, Je - sus, stands With all - en - gag - ing charms;

Hark, how He calls His ten - der lambs, And folds them in His arms.

2 Permit them to approach, He cries,
  Nor scorn their humble name;
  For 'twas to bless such souls as these
  The Lord of angels came.

3 He'll lead us to the heavenly streams
  Where living waters flow,
  And guide us to the fruitful fields
  Where trees of knowledge grow.

4 The feeblest lamb amid the flock
  Shall be its Shepherd's care;
  While folded in the Saviour's arms,
  We're safe from every snare.

42. Kindness. C. M.

1 SPEAK gently: it is better far
  To rule by love than fear;
  Speak gently, let no harsh word mar
  The good we may do here.

2 Speak gently to the young, for they
  Will have enough to bear;
  Pass through this life as best they may,
  'Tis full of anxious care.

3 Speak gently to the aged one,
  Grieve not the careworn heart;
  The sands of life are nearly run,
  Let them in peace depart.

4 Speak gently to the erring ones,
  They must have toiled in vain;
  Perchance unkindness made them so,
  Oh, win them back again.

43. Charity. C. M.

1 FOUNTAIN of good, to own Thy love
  Our thankful hearts incline;
  What can we render, Lord, to Thee,
  When all the worlds are Thine?

2 But Thou hast needy brethren here,
  Partakers of Thy grace,
  Whose names Thou wilt Thyself confess
  Before the Father's face.

3 And in their accents of distress
  Thy pleading voice is heard;
  In them Thou mayst be clothed and fed,
  And visited, and cheered.

4 Thy face with reverence and with love
  We in Thy poor would see;
  Oh, may we minister to them,
  And in them, Lord, to Thee.

44. Children's Friend. C. M.

1 Thou Guardian of our youthful days,
To Thee our prayers ascend ;
To Thee we'll tune our songs of praise,
Jesus, the children's Friend.

2 From Thee our daily mercies flow,
Our life and health descend ;
Oh, save our souls from sin and wo ;
Thou art the children's Friend.

3 Teach us to prize Thy holy word
And to its truths attend ;
Thus shall we learn to fear the Lord,
And love the children's Friend.

4 Oh, may we feel a Saviour's love,
To Him our souls commend,
Who left His glorious throne above
To be the children's Friend.

45. Whitsun-day. C. M.

1 When God of old came down from heaven,
In power and wrath He came !
Before His feet the clouds were riven,
Half darkness and half flame ;

2 But when He came the second time,
He came in power and love ;
Softer than gale at morning prime
Hovered His holy Dove.

3 The fires, that rushed on Sinai down
In sudden torrents dread,
Now gently light, a glorious crown,
On every sainted head.

4 And as on Israel's awe-struck ear
The voice exceeding loud,
The trump, that angels quake to hear,
Thrilled from the deep, dark cloud :

5 So, when the Spirit of our God
Came down his flock to find,
A voice from heaven was heard abroad,
A rushing, mighty wind.

6 It fills the Church of God ; it fills
The sinful world around ;
Only in stubborn hearts and wills
No place for it is found.

46. Whitsun-day. C. M.

1 He's come, let every knee be bent,
All hearts new joy resume ;
Sing, ye redeem'd with one consent,
" The Comforter is come."

2 What greater gift, what greater love,
Could God on man bestow ?
Angels for this rejoice above,
Let man rejoice below.

3 Hail, blessed Spirit ! may each soul
Thy sacred influence feel :
Do Thou each sinful thought contro',
And fix our wavering zeal.

4 Thou to the conscience dost convey
Those checks which we should know,
Thy motions point to us the way ;
Thou giv'st us strength to go. Amen.

47. Militant. C. M.

1 The Son of God goes forth to war,
A kingly crown to gain ;
His blood-red banner streams afar :
Who follows in His train ?

2 Who best can drink His cup of woe,
Triumphant over pain ;
Who patient bears His cross below,
He follows in His train.

3 The martyr first, whose eagle eye
Could pierce beyond the grave ;
Who saw his Master in the sky,
And call'd on Him to save.

4 Like Him, with pardon on His tongue,
In midst of mortal pain ;
He prayed for them that did the wrong
Who followed in His train ?

5 A glorious band, the chosen few,
On whom the Spirit came ;   [knew,
Twelve valiant saints, their hope they
And mock'd the cross and flame.

6 They climb'd the steep ascent of heaven
Through peril, toil, and pain ;
O God ! to us may grace be given
To follow in their train. Amen.

48. FAITH. S. M.

Arr. from HAYDN.

1. How gen - tle God's com - mands! How kind his precepts are!

Come, cast your burdens on the Lord, And trust his constant care.

2 His bounty will provide,
    His saints securely dwell ;
That hand that bears creation up,
    Shall guard His children well.

3 His goodness stands approved,
    Unchanged from day to day ;
I'll drop my burden at His feet,
    And bear a song away.

49. S. M.

1 I was a wandering sheep,
    I did not love the fold ;
I did not love my Shepherd's voice,
    I would not be controlled.

2 I was a wayward child,
    I did not love my home ;
I did not love my Father's voice,
    I loved afar to roam.

3 The Shepherd sought his sheep,
    The Father sought his child,
And followed me o'er vale and hill,
    O'er deserts waste and wild.

4 He found me nigh to death,
    Famished, and faint, and lone ;

He bound me with the bands of love,
    And saved the wandering one.

50. Sunday. S. M.

1 This is a day of light ;
    Let there be light to-day ;
O Day-spring, rise upon our night,
    And chase its gloom away.

2 This is a day of rest :
    Our failing strength renew !
On weary brain and troubled breast
    Shed Thou Thy freshening dew.

3 This is the day of peace :
    Thy peace our spirits fill ;
Bid Thou the blast of discord cease,
    The waves of strife be still.

4 This is the day of prayer :
    Let earth and heaven draw near ;
Lift up our hearts to seek Thee there ;
    Come down to meet us here.

5 This is the first of days :
    Send forth Thy quickening breath,
And wake dead souls to love and praise,
    O Vanquisher of death !

51. Festal Hymn. S. M.

1 REJOICE, ye pure in heart,
Rejoice, give thanks and sing;
Your festal banner wave on high,
The Cross of Christ your King.

2 Bright youth and snow-crowned age,
Strong men and maidens meek,
Raise high your free exulting song,
God's wondrous praises speak.

3 With all the angel choirs,
With all the saints on earth,
Pour out the strains of joy and bliss,
True rapture, noblest mirth.

4 Your clear Hosannas raise,
And Alleluias loud;
Whilst answering echoes upward float,
Like wreaths of incense cloud.

5 With voice as full and strong
As ocean's surging praise,

Send forth the hymns our fathers loved,
The psalms of ancient days.

6 Yes, on, through life's long path,
Still chanting as they go,
From youth to age, by night and day,
In gladness and in woe.

7 Still lift your standard high,
Still march in firm array,
As warriors through the darkness toil,
Till dawns the golden day.

8 At last the march shall end,
The wearied ones shall rest,
The pilgrims find the Father's House,
Jerusalem the blest.

9 Then on, ye pure in heart,
Rejoice, give thanks, and sing;
Your festal banner wave on high,
The Cross of Christ your King.

52. ADRIAN. S. M.

J. E. GOULD.

1. Se - rene I laid me down, Be - neath God's guard - ian care;

I slept, and I a - woke and found My kind Pre-serv - er near.

2 Oh how shall I repay
The bounties of my God?
This feeble spirit pants beneath
The pleasing, painful load.

3 Dear Saviour, to thy cross
I bring my sacrifice;
Sprinkled with blood, it shall ascend
With fragrance to the skies.

53. YARNDLEY. III. 1.

1. Words are things of lit - tle cost, Quick-ly spok - en, quick-ly lost;

We for - get them, but they stand Wit - nes - ses at God's right hand.

2 Oh, how often ours have been
Idle words, and words of sin!
Grant us, Lord, from day to day,
Strength to watch, and grace to pray:

3 May our lips, from sin kept free,
Love to speak and sing of Thee;
Till in heaven we learn to raise
Songs of everlasting praise.

54. Trinity.

1 HOLY Father! hear our cry;
Holy Saviour! bend Thine ear;
Holy Spirit! come Thou nigh;
Father, Saviour, Spirit, hear.

2 Father, save us from our sin;
Saviour, we Thy mercy crave;
Gracious Spirit, make us clean:
Father, Son, and Spirit, save.

3 Father, Son, and Spirit—Thou
One Jehovah—shed abroad
All Thy grace within us now:
Be our Father and our God.

55. Jesus, Saviour.

1 JESUS, Saviour, Son of God,
Who for me life's pathway trod,
Who for me became a child;
Make me humble, meek, and mild.

2 I Thy little lamb would be,
Jesus, I would follow Thee;
Samuel was Thy child of old,
Take me, too, within Thy fold.

3 Teach me how to pray to Thee,
Make me holy, heavenly:
Let me love what Thou dost love,
Let me live alone with Thee.

56. INDIANA. III. 1.

DONNIZETTL.

1. God is love! the sil - ver brook, Murm'ring in its sha - dy nook,

Sings the song, in soft - est tones, As it rip - ples o'er the stones.

Duet.

God is love! each ti - ny flower Swells the prais - es of His power,

As it blooms in beau - ty rare, Shed-ding fra - grance on the air.

2 God is love! in every breeze,
Rustling through the forest trees;
We the still small voice may hear,
Whisp'ring of His presence near;

God is love! the little birds
Carol forth with joyous words;
Let us join the grateful song,
Praises to our God belong.

57. Easter.

1 WE will carol joyfully,
On this holy festal day ;
To our risen Lord and King
Grateful homage we will bring.

2 We will carol joyfully,
As with sweet accord we bring
Praise from every heart and voice
To our risen Lord and King.

3 We will carol joyfully,
While our love and thanks we give
To our risen Lord and King,
Him who died that we might live.

4 We will carol joyfully,
And to Him our offerings bring,—
Grateful hearts with love and praise,
To our risen Lord and King.

58. VINEYARD. Christmas.

By permission of
REV. A. B. GOODRICH, D. D.

1. In the vine-yard of our Fa-ther, Dai-ly work we find to do;

Scattered gleanings we may gather, Though we are but young and few;

Lit-tle clus-ters, Lit-tle clus-ters Help to fill the garners, too.

2 Toiling early in the morning,
　　Catching moments through the day,
Nothing small or lowly scorning,
　　So along our path we stray;
　　　　Gathering gladly
　　Free-will offerings by the way.

3 Not for selfish praise or glory,
　　Not for objects nothing worth—
But to send the blessed story
　　Of the Gospel o'er the earth,—
　　　　Telling mortals
　　Of our Lord and Saviour's birth.

59. WORK, FOR THE NIGHT IS COMING.

By permission from "Song Garden."

1. Work, for the night is com - ing, Work thro' the morning hours,

Work while the dew is spark - ling, Work 'mid springing flow'rs;

Work when the day grows bright - er, Work in the glow - ing sun;

Work, for the night is com - ing, When man's work is done.

2 Work, for the night is coming,
 Work through the sunny noon;
Fill brightest hours with labor,
 Rest comes sure and soon;
Give every flying minute
 Something to keep in store;
Work, for the night is coming,
 When man works no more.

3 Work, for the night is coming,
 Under the sunset skies;
While their bright tints are glowing,
 Work, for daylight flies;
Work till the last beam fadeth,
 Fadeth to shine no more;
Work while the night is dark'ning,
 When man's work is o'er.

62. DIES IRÆ.   Advent. (Burial of the Dead.)   J. H. W.

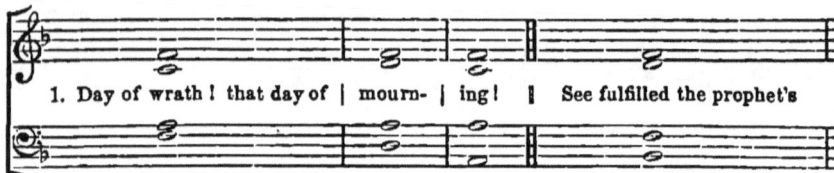

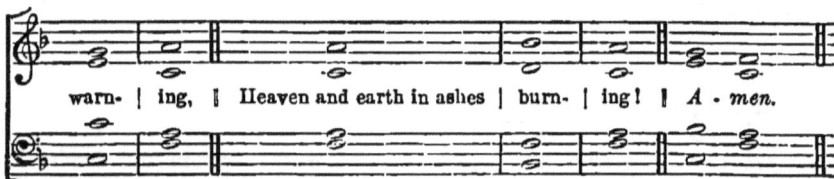

1. Day of wrath ! that day of | mourn- | ing ! | See fulfilled the prophet's

warn- | ing, | Heaven and earth in ashes | burn- | ing ! | A - men.

2 Oh, what fear man's bosom rendeth,
When from heav'n the Judge descendeth,
On whose sentence all dependeth !

3 Wondrous sound the trumpet flingeth,
Through earth's sepulchres it ringeth,
All before the Throne it bringeth.

4 Death is struck, and nature quaking,
All creation is awaking,
To its Judge an answer making.

5 Lo, the Book exactly worded,
Wherein all hath been recorded !
Thence shall judgment be awarded.

6 When the Judge His seat attaineth,
And each hidden deed arraigneth,
Nothing unavenged remaineth.

7 What shall I, frail man, be pleading,
Who for me be interceding,
When the just are mercy needing ?

8 King of majesty tremendous,
Who dost free salvation send us,
Fount of pity, then befriend us.

9 Think, good Jesu, my salvation
Caused Thy wondrous Incarnation ;
Leave me not to reprobation.

10 Faint and weary Thou hast sought me,
On the Cross of suffering bought me ;
Shall such grace be vainly brought me ?

11 Righteous Judge ! for sin's pollution
Grant Thy gift of absolution,
Ere that day of retribution. ,

12 Guilty, now I pour my moaning,
All my shame with anguish owning ;
Spare, O God, Thy suppliant groaning.

13 Thou the sinful woman savedest ;
Thou the dying thief forgavest ;
And to me a hope vouchsafest.

14 Worthless are my prayers and sighing,
Yet, good Lord, in grace complying,
Rescue me from fires undying.

15 With Thy favored sheep O place me,
Not among the goats abase me ;
But to Thy right hand upraise me.

16 While the wicked are confounded,
Doomed to flames of woe unbounded,
Call me, with Thy saints surrounded.

17 Low I kneel, with heart submission ;
See, like ashes, my contrition ;
Help me in my last condition.

18 Ah ! that day of tears and mourning !
From the dust of earth returning,
Man for judgment must prepare him ;

19 Spare, O God, in mercy spare him !
Lord, all pitying, Jesu blest,
Grant them Thine eternal rest.   Amen.

63. ADVENT.

Rev. R. N. P.

1. Lo! He comes in clouds de - scend - ing, Once for fa - vor'd sin - ners slain; Thou-sand thou-sand saints at - tend - ing Swell the tri - umph of His train: Al - le - lu - ia! Al - le - lu - ia! Christ ap - pears on earth a - gain. A - - - - men.

2 Every eye shall now behold Him
  Robed in dread majesty;
They who set at naught and sold Him,
  Pierced and nailed Him to the tree,
    Deeply wailing,
  Shall the true Messiah see.

3 Those dear tokens of His passion
  Still His dazzling Body bears;
Cause of endless exultation
  To His ransomed worshippers;
    With what rapture
  Gaze we on those glorious scars.

4 Yea, Amen, let all adore Thee,
  High on Thine eternal throne;
Saviour, take the power and glory:
  Claim the kingdoms for Thine own;
    Oh, come quickly!
  Alleluia! Amen.

64. ADVENT.　Anthem.

ISA. xv. 8.　　　　　　　　　　　　　　　　　MACFARREN.

Drop down, ye heav- ens, from a - bove, and let　the　skies　pour down

right-eousness: Let.... the earth ..... o - - pen, and let them

bring forth sal - va - - - tion. A - - - men.　　A - - men.

A - men. A - - - - men.

65. ANY HOLYDAY ANTHEM.

PS. xxxiv. 8.　　　　　　　　　　　　　　　　MACFARREN.

Oh, taste and see how gra - cious is　the Lord: See!　see　how

gra - cious is the Lord; Oh, taste and see how gra - cious

is the Lord, how gra - cious, gra - cious is the Lord.

Bless-ed is the man that trust-eth in Him, Bless- ed is the

man that trust-eth in Him. Oh, taste and see how gra - cious

is....... the Lord, how gra - cious how gra - cious is the Lord.

66. CHRISTMAS. Anthem.

HYMN 45.   REV. R. N. P.

1. Hark! the he - rald an - gels sing, Glo - ry to the new - born King;

Peace on earth, and mer - cy mild; God and sin - ners re - con - ciled.

2 Joyful all ye nations rise,
Join the triumph of the skies;
With th' angelic host proclaim,
Christ is born in Bethlehem!

3 Christ, by highest heaven adored,
Christ, the everlasting Lord,
Late in time behold Him come,
Offspring of the Virgin's womb.

4 Veiled in flesh, the Godhead see:
Hail th' incarnate Deity,
Pleased, as man, with man to dwell;
Jesus, now Emmanuel.

5 Risen with healing in His wings,
Light and life to all He brings,
Hail the Sun of righteousness!
Hail the heaven-born Prince of Peace!

67. CHRISTMAS CAROL.

1. Good King Wenceslas looked out, On the Feast of Ste - phen;

When the snow lay round a - bout, Deep, and crisp, and e - ven;

Brightly shone the moon that night, Tho' the frost was cru - el,

When a poor man came in sight, Gath'ring win - ter fu - - el.

2 " Hither, page, and stand by me,
  If thou know'st it, telling,
Yonder peasant, who is he?
  Where and what his dwelling?"
" Sire, he lives a good league hence,
  Underneath the mountain;
Right against the forest fence,
  By Saint Agnes' fountain."

3 " Bring me flesh, and bring me wine,
  Bring me pine-logs hither;
Thou and I will see him dine,
  When we bear them thither."
Page and monarch forth they went,
  Forth they went together:
Through the rude wind's wild lament
  And the bitter weather.

4 " Sire, the night is darker now,
  And the wind blows stronger;
Fails my heart I know not how;
  I can go no longer."
" Mark my footsteps, good my page,
  Tread thou in them boldly:
Thou shalt find the winter's rage
  Freeze thy blood less coldly."

5 In his master's steps he trod,
  Where the snow lay dinted;
Heat was in the very sod
  Which the Saint had printed.
Therefore, Christian men, be sure,
  Wealth or rank possessing,
Ye who now will bless the poor
  Shall yourselves find blessing.

68. CHRISTMAS CAROL.   *"Nowell" means "Good News."*

1. The first Now-ell, the An-gel did say, Was to three poor shepherds in fields as they lay; In fields where they lay keeping their sheep, In a cold winter's night that was so deep. Now-ell, Now-ell, Now-ell, Now-ell, Born is the King of Is-ra-el.

2 They lookéd up and saw a Star,
Shining in the East, beyond them far,
And to the earth it gave great light,
And so it continued both day and night.

3 And by the light of that same Star,
Three Wise Men came from country far ;
To seek for a King was their intent,
And follow the Star wherever it went.

4 This Star drew nigh to the north-west,
O'er Bethlehem it took its rest,

And there it did both stop and stay,
Right over the place where Jesus lay.

5 Then enter'd in those Wise Men three,
Most reverently upon their knee,
And offer'd there, in His presence,
Both gold, and myrrh, and frankincense.

6 Then let us all with one accord,
Sing praises to our Heavenly Lord,
That hath made heaven and earth of nought,
And with His blood mankind hath bought.

69. HERE IS JOY. Christmas Carol.

1. Here is joy for ev-ery age, Ev-ery ge-ne-ra-tion;

Prince and pea-sant, chief and sage, Ev-ery tongue and na-tion:

Ev-ery tongue and na-tion, Ev-ery rank and sta-tion,

Hath to-day sal-va-tion: Al-le-lu-ia!........

2 When the world drew near its close,
   Came our Lord and Leader;
 From the Lily sprang the Rose,
   From the Bush the Cedar;
 From the Bush the Cedar,
 From the judg'd the Pleader,
 From the faint the Feeder:
     Alleluia!

3 God, that came on earth this morn,
   In a manger lying,
 Hallowed birth by being born,
   Vanquished death by dying;
 Vanquished death by dying,
 Rallied back the flying,
 Ended sin and sighing:
     Alleluia!

70. THE SNOW LAY ON THE GROUND.   G. W. W.

1. The snow lay on the ground, The stars shone bright, When Christ our

Lord was born on Christ - mas night. Ve - ni - te a - do -

re - mus Do - mi - num, Ve - ni - te a - do - re - mus

Chorus.

Do - ni - num. Ve - ni - te a - do - re - mus Do - mi -

num, Ve - ni - te a - do - re - mus Do - mi - num.

2 'Twas Mary, Virgin pure,
Of holy life,
That brought into this world
The God-made man.
She laid Him in a stall
At Bethlehem ;
The ass and oxen shared
The roof with them.

3 Saint Joseph, too, was by
To tend the Child ;
To guard Him, and protect
His mother, mild.

The angels hover'd round,
And sung this song,
Venite adoremus
Dominum !

4 And then that manger, poor,
Became a throne,
For He whom Mary bore
Was God, the Son.
Oh, come then, let us join
The Heavenly Host,
To praise the Father, Son,
And Holy Ghost.

71. CHRISTMAS CAROL.

Mrs. T. I. Holcombe.

1. Bright, bright in sil-ver light The morning stars are shin-ing, And
shep-herds watch-ing o'er their flocks, Were on their staves re-
clin - - - ing, Were on their staves re-clin - - - ing.

2 Clear! clear! so very near,
A burst of music sounding,
That flocks and shepherds rose at once
With swelling hearts rebounding.

3 Loud! loud! the chorus greet,
Till all the air was swelling,
And from the heavens came a voice,
That joyful news was telling.

4 Peace! peace! on earth be peace,
Good will to brothers greeting,
Arise and hasten to the Babe,
Fast in the manger sleeping.

5 Joy! joy! a Child is born,
Foretold in ancient story,
Born to redeem our souls from sin,
'Tis Christ the Lord of glory.

72. ANGELS OF JESUS. Christmas.

1. Hark! hark, my soul; An-gel-ic songs are swell-ing O'er earth's green fields, and o-cean's wave-beat shore: How sweet the truth those blessed strains are tell-ing Of that new life when sin shall be no more.

Chorus.

An-gels of Je-sus, An-gels of light, Sing-ing to wel-come the pilgrims of the night.

2 Onward we go, for still we hear them singing,
    " Come, weary souls, for Jesus bids you come :"
And, through the dark its echoes sweetly ringing,
    The music of the Gospel leads us home.
Cho. Angels of Jesus, Angels of light,
    Singing to welcome the pilgrims of the night.

3 Far, far away, like bells at evening pealing,
 The voice of Jesus sounds o'er land and sea,
 And laden souls by thousands meekly stealing,
 Kind Shepherd, turn their steps to Thee.—*Chorus.*

4 Rest comes at length, though life be long and dreary
 The day must dawn, and darksome night be passed ;
 Faith's journey ends in welcome to the weary,
 And heaven, the heart's true home, will come at last.—*Chorus.*

Sing, Angels, sing on! your faithful watches keeping ;
 Till morning's sweet fragments of the songs above;
 And life's long shadows shall end the night of weeping,
 In cloudless love.—*Chorus.*

73. LITTLE CHILDREN, CAN YOU TELL. Christmas.

1. Lit - tle chil - dren, can you tell? Do you know the
2. Yes, we know the sto - ry well; Lis - ten now, and

sto - ry well? Ev - ery girl and ev - ery boy, Why the an - gels
hear us tell, Ev - ery girl and ev - ery boy, Why the an - gels

Chorus.

sing for joy On the Christ-mas morn - - ing?
sing for joy On the Christ-mas morn - - ing.

3 Shepherds sat upon the ground,
Fleecy flocks were scattered round,
When a brightness filled the sky,
And a voice was heard on high
On the Christmas morning.

4 "Joy and peace," the angels sang,
Far the pleasant echoes rang;
"Peace on earth! to men good will!"
Hark! the angels sing it still
On the Christmas morning.

5 For a little Babe that day
Cradled in a manger lay;
Born on earth our Lord to be;
This the wondering angels see
On the Christmas morning.

6 Joy our little hearts shall fill,
Peace and love, and all good-will;
This fair Babe of Bethlehem
Children loves, and bless them
On the Christmas morning.

74. LUTHER'S CHRISTMAS HYMN. Tune—"*Frank*," 33.

1 FROM heaven above to earth I come,
To bring glad news to every home;
Glad tidings of great joy I bring,
Whereof I now shall say and sing.

2 To you, this night, is born a child,
Of Mary, chosen mother mild;
This little child of lowly birth
Shall be the joy of all the earth.

3 He brings those blessings, long ago
Prepared by God for all below;
Henceforth His kingdom open stands
To you, as to the angel bands.

4 Now let us all with gladsome cheer
Follow the shepherds, and draw near
Who is this child so young and fair?
The blessed Christ-child lieth here.

5 My heart for very joy doth leap,
My lips no more can silence keep;
I, too, will sing with joyful tongue,
That sweetest ancient cradle song.

6 Glory to God in highest heaven,
Who unto man his Son has given!
While angels sing with pious mirth,
A glad New Year to all the earth!

75. THE ANGEL CHORUS. Christmas.

Duet.—SOPRANO AND BASS.   *Words and Music by* Jr.

1. On the win-try and lone-ly hill-side, All in the dim star-light,

Shepherds o-ver the flock were keep-ing Watch at the dead of night;

Trio.—SOPRANO, ALTO, AND BASS.

When swift angels of light came down, And earth with ho - san - nas rang;

Harps of gold and che-ru-bic voi - ces Loud-ly and cheerly sang At Beth-le-hem:

Chorus.

Glo - ry to God in the high - est, And on earth peace, good - will to men.

2 Earth was wrapped in a robe of winter:
　　Kindly the new-fall'n snow
Drew the veil of a virgin whiteness
　　Pure over guilt and woe.
Beasts of prey on the frozen mountain,
　　Flocks on the charmed plain,
Nature all, in entranced rapture,
　　Listened to that sweet strain
　　　From Bethlehem :—
　　　　Glory to God, &c.

3 Proudly marching along the forum,
　　Priests with a pompous train,
Closed the gates of the Roman Janus
　　Under a Cæsar's reign.
Every where, and in every nation,
　　War, with its carnage grim,
Shouts and groans, and the roar of battle,
　　Ceased for the Angel's hymn
　　　At Bethlehem :—
　　　　Glory to God, &c.

4 Lo ! each oracle of the heathen
　　Soon disenchanted proves:
Through the gloom of the dark Dodona,
　　Dumb are the oaken groves ;
Dumb the voice of Apollo's priestess,
　　Delphi is left forlorn :
All the realms of the demons tremble,
　　Knowing their Conqueror born
　　　At Bethlehem:—
　　　　Glory to God, &c.

5 Wide and wider at every Christmas
　　Echoes the joyful sound ;
From Judea the glad good tidings
　　Now run the wide world round.
Sing, then sing, for the listening Angels,
　　Bending on eager wing,
Join us now in the royal chorus
　　They were the first to sing
　　　At Bethlehem :— '
　　　　Glory to God, &c.

76. THE CHILDREN IN THE TEMPLE. Christmas.

REV. DR. OGILBY.　　　　　　　　　　　　DR. H. S. CUTLER.

1. Ho - san - na to King David's Son, De - scend - ed from the

Accomp.

heav'nly throne; In Christmas songs we hail his birth, Who brought sal-vation

Chorus.

to the earth. Ho - san - na to King David's Son!

Ho - san - na to King David's Son! Ho - san - na in the

high-est!

Chimes.

2.
Hosanna to the new-born Child,
Of virgin mother, meek and mild!
In manger cradle see Him laid,
By whom the earth and heavens were made.

Cho.—Hosanna to the wonderful!
    Hosanna to the wonderful!
    Hosanna in the highest!

3.
Hosanna to the incarnate Word,
In Bethlehem born! The mighty God!
Our hearts and tongues with joy should raise
Their glad hosannas to His praise!

Cho.—Hosanna to the mighty God!
    Hosanna to the mighty God!
    Hosanna in the highest!

4.
With shepherds on Judea's plains,
With Angels in their nobler strains;
Let our hosannas joyful rise
To join the anthems of the skies!

Cho.—Hosanna, everlasting Father!
    Hosanna, everlasting Father!
    Hosanna in the highest!

5.
Let every nation, every voice,
In merry Christmas songs rejoice;
Both old and young with gladness sing,
That Christ is born to be our King!

Cho.—Hosanna to the Prince of Peace!
    Hosanna to the Prince of Peace!
    Hosanna in the highest!

77. A SHEPHERD BAND.

PRÆTORIUS, 1609.

1. A shepherd band their flocks.... are keep-ing, And gen - tle lambs are sweet-ly sleep-ing; When sud-den-ly they all be - hold............... An an - gel in bright robes,.... with harp.... of gold.

2 Glad tidings of great joy he bringeth
The azure vault with anthems ringeth:
"Immanuel" awakes the song, [long.
And countless hosts the glorious theme pro-

3 "To you, this day, is born a Saviour,
Your Prophet, Priest, and King forever;
All glory be to God," they cry;
"All glory be to God," let earth reply.

4 "On earth be peace with mercy blending,
Good will to men, and love unending;"
Thus sweetly sing the angel throng,
And all the heavenly host rehearse the song.

5 Thro' field and wood the song resoundeth,
O'er hill and vale the chorus boundeth:

Exultingly the echoes roll, [pole.
And hymns of triumph spread from pole to

6 The shepherds view the host returning,
Their hearts with holy ardor burning,
To Bethlehem they wend their way,
Repeating with glad tongues th' angelic lay

7 In haste they seek the heavenly Stranger;
They find the Babe laid in a manger;
With wonder and with awe they fall,
And joyfully adore Him, Lord of all!

8 Now every voice with rapture swelleth,
For Christ the Lord with mortals dwelleth:
Let men and angels Him adore,
And shout their loud hosannas evermore.

78. EPIPHANY.

MOZART.

1. { Saw ye nev-er in the twilight, When the sun had left the skies,
Up in heav'n the clear stars shining, Thro' the gloom like sil-ver eyes? }

So of old, the wise men watching, Saw a lit-tle stranger star,

And they knew the King was giv-en, And they fol-lowed it from far.

2 Heard ye never of the story,
    How they cross'd the desert wild,
  Journey'd on by plain and mountain,
    Till they found the Holy Child?
  How they open'd all their treasure,
    Kneeling to that Infant King,
  Gave the gold and fragrant incense,
    Gave the myrrh in offering?

3 Know ye not that lowly Baby
    Was the bright and morning Star,
  He who came to light the Gentiles
    And the darkened isle afar?
  And we too may seek His cradle,
    There our hearts' best treasures bring,
  Love, and Faith, and true devotion,
    For our Saviour, God, and King.

79. EPIPHANY ANTHEM.

ISAIAH lii. 7.

How beau - ti - ful up - on the mount-ains, How beau - ti - ful up - on the

mount - ains, How beau - ti - ful up-on the mountains are the feet of

him.... that bring-eth good tid - ings, that pub - lish - eth peace, that

pub - lish - eth peace, that bring-eth good tid - ings, good tid - ings of good, that

pub - lisheth sal - va - tion, that saith un - to Zi - on, thy God reigneth,

thy God reign - eth. Break forth in - to joy, sing to - gether,

sing to - geth - er, ye waste places of Je - ru - sa - lem, for the

Lord hath com - fort - ed his peo - ple, He hath re - deem - ed Je -

ru - sa - lem. Hal - le - lu - jah! Hal - le - lu - jah! Praise ye the

Lord. Hal - le - lu - jah! Hal - le - lu - jah! Praise ye the Lord.

90. ALLELUIA. Easter.   *Words by* REV. MARCUS LANE

Chorus.

Christ is ris - en! Al - le - lu - ia! Ris - en our vic - torious Head!

Fine.

Sing His prai - ses! Al - le - lu - ia! Christ is ris - en from the dead!

1. All the doubt - ing and de - jec - tion Of our trembling hearts have ceased,

D. C.

'Tis His day of re - sur - rec - tion, Let us rise and keep the feast.

2 Christ is risen! henceforth never
   Death or hell shall us enthrall;
   Be with Christ, in Him forever
   We have triumphed over all.—*Cho.*

3 Gratefully our hearts adore Him,
   As His light once more appears,

Bowing down in joy before Him,
   Rising up from grief and tears.—*Cho.*

4 Death and hell before Him bending,
   He doth rise the Victor now;
   Angels on His steps attending,
   Glory round His wounded brow.—*Cho.*

81. LENT. Litany. PEARCE.

1. God the Father, | God the Son, || Holy Ghost the | Com - fort - er,

Ever Blessèd.... | Three in One; || Spare us, Holy... | Tri - ni - ty.

A - men.

2 Christ, Whose mercy | guideth still
Sinners from the | paths of ill,
Rule our hearts, our | spirits fill;
Hear us, | Holy Jesu.

3 Thou Who on the | Cross didst reign,
Dying there in | bitter pain,
Cleansing with Thy | blood our stain;
Hear us, | Holy Jesu.

4 Thou Whose will it is that we
Should from death re- | turn to Thee,
And should live e- | ternally;
Hear us, | Holy Jesu.

5 Shepherd of the | straying sheep,
Comforter of | them that weep,
Hear us crying | from the deep;
Hear us, | Holy Jesu.

6 In all pover- | ty and wealth,
In all sickness | and in health,
Ever from the | Tempter's stealth;
Save us, | Holy Jesu.

7 For all lack of | love and faith,
From a sudden. | evil death,
Thou Whose Arm de- | livereth
Save us, | Holy Jesu.

8 When our dying | draweth near;
On the last Great | Day of fear,
Master, King, Re- | deemer dear;
Save us, | Holy Jesu.

9 That in Thy pure | innocence
We may wash our | soul's offence,
And find truest | penitence;
We beseech | Thee, — Jesu.

10 That we give to | sin no place,
That we never | quench Thy grace,
That we ever | seek Thy Face;
We beseech | Thee, — Jesu.

11 That denying | evil lust,
Living godly, | meek, and just,
In Thee only | we may trust;
We beseech | Thee, — Jesu.

12 That to sin for | ever dead,
We may live to | Thee instead,
And the narrow | pathway tread;
We beseech | Thee, — Jesu.

13 When shall end the | battle sore,
When onr pilgri- | mage is o'er,
Grant Thy peace for | evermore;
We beseech | Thee, — Jesu.

82. PALM SUNDAY.

J. H. W.

Boys. Girls. Both.

Ho - san - na, Ho - san - na, Ho - san - na, Praise ye the Lord.

Duet.

1. What are those soul-re - viv - ing strains Which ech-o thus from Sa-lem's plains?

Chorus.

What anthems loud and loud-er still, So sweet-ly sound from Zi - on's hill?

2 Lo! 'tis an infant chorus sings
 Hosannas to the King of kings;
 The Saviour comes, and babes proclaim
 Salvation in Emanuel's Name.

3 Chief Priests and scribes their murmurs raise,
 But Jesus owns the children's praise;
 And now they make the temple ring,
 With shouts of welcome to their King.

4 Messiah's Name shall joy impart,
 Alike to Jew and Gentile heart;
 We, too, would join in that glad song,
 And evermore the strain prolong.

83. WORGAN. Easter.

1. Je - sus Christ has risen to - day, Al - - - - le - lu - ia!

Our tri - umphant ho - ly day, Al - - - - le - lu - - ia!

Who did once up - on the Cross Al - - - - - le - lu - - ia.

Suf - fer to re - deem our loss. Al - - - le - lu - - ia! A-men.

2 Hymns of praise then let us sing   Alleluia!
Unto Christ, our heavenly King,   Alleluia!
Who endured the Cross and Grave,   Alleluia!
Sinners to redeem and save.   Alleluia!

But the pain which He endured   Alleluia!
Our salvation hath procured;   Alleluia!
Now above the sky He's King,   Alleluia!
Where the angels ever sing.   Alleluia!   Amen.

84. EASTER ANTHEM.

1. Christ the Lord　　is ris'n to-day,　　Hal-le-lu-jah! hal-le-lu-jah!

Sons of men and an-gels say; Raise your joys　and triumphs high,

Hal-le-lu-jah! hal-le-lu-jah! Sing, ye heavens, and earth re-ply.

Omit in *last* verse, and go to *

Hal-le-lu-jah! Hal-le-lu-jah! Hal-le-lu-jah!

*After the last verse.

And He shall reign for ev-er and ev-er, for ev-er and ev-er,

Hal - le - lu - jah! hal - le - lu - jah! Hal - le - lu - jah!

Adagio.

2 Love's redeeming work is done,
Fought the fight, the victory won;
Jesus' agony is o'er,
Darkness veils the earth no more.

3 Vain the stone, the watch, the seal,
Christ has burst the gates of hell;

Death in vain forbids Him rise,
Christ hath opened paradise.

4 Soar we now where Christ hath led,
Following our exalted Head:
Made like Him, like Him we rise;
Ours the cross, the grave, the skies.
And He shall reign for ever, &c.

85. EASTER CAROL.

Words by Rt. Rev. A. C. Coxe, D.D.   J. H. W.

Duet.   *Fine.*

1. { How in the flow-'ry Spring, my God, The buds of prom - ise ope, }
   { And blos - som o'er life's thor - ny road, To cheer the Christian's hope! }
D. c. And flour - ish in im - mor - tal bloom, In E - dens of the skies.

Like them, ex - ult - ing from the tomb, We, too, re - vived, shall rise,

D. C.

2 What though in pensive Autumn's wane,
Earth's sere grown glories fall,
And sleep through Winter's dull domain,
When death is writ on all;
Exulting, in the breaking year,
The lily doth unclose
And daisies o'er the waste appear,
And roses from the snows.

3 So then to dust, our dust shall turn,
So too shall rise and sing,
When falls upon the mouldered urn
The joyous dew of Spring;
The God that rears the tender flowers,
And breathes to life their dust,
From the cold grave will quicken ours,
And new-create the just.

86. JESUS LIVES. Easter Carol.

GEORGE D. WILDES.   *By permission of* E. P. D. & Co.

1. Je - sus lives! O Day of Days! Glad we bring our grate - ful praise;

He is ris - en! Gone the gloom, An - gels sit with-in the tomb.

Vain the taunt of Jew de - ny - ing, Vain the vaunt o'er Je - sus dy - ing,

rall.

Heavenly voi - ces, from the grave, Now proclaim His pow'r to save.

a tempo.

1, 2 & 3. He is ris - en! Come and see, How He triumphed migh - ti - ly!

Conqueror thus o'er all His foes, Je - sus from the dead a - rose.

2 Lord and Prophet, spake He not?
Have ye His own words forgot,
Telling, while in Galilee,
Thus the victory should be?
How through scorn and dire affliction,
Thorny way and crucifixion,
Vanquished Death, and rent the grave,—
Christ the King should live to save.

Cho. He is risen! Come, &c.

3 Tearful to the sepulcher
Mary comes in grief and fear;
Sees the stone now rolled away,
Hears the waiting angels say:
"Why the dead among the living
Seek ye?" Lo! the Lord Life-giving

Rises! vain the watch, the grave:
Prince of Life, He lives to save!
Cho. He is risen! Come, &c.

4 Welcome then, the Day of Days!
Lord 'tis Thine our tuneful praise;
Thine, for us, the Tempted, Tried,
Thine, for us, the Crucified;
Thine for us the Resurrection,
Thine the Life, the Sure Protection.
Saviour! Sovereign o'er the grave,
May we know Thy pow'r to save.

Cho. He is risen! joyfully,
Lord! we raise our song to Thee,
Conqueror thus o'er all His foes,
Jesus from the dead arose.

87. EASTER ANTHEM.
Ps. cxviii. 24.   MACFARREN.

This is the day which the Lord hath made, This is the day, This is the day,........ This is the day which the Lord hath made; let us re-

joice, let us re-joice, let us re-joice, and be glad in it.

GLORIA PATRI. (*For No. 87.*)   Rev. R. N. P.

Glo-ry be to the Fa-ther, and to the Son, and

to the Ho-ly Ghost; As it was in the be-gin-ning, is

now, and ev-er shall be, world without end...... A-men. A-men.

88. EASTER CAROL.   *Words by* REV. MARCUS LANE.

Chorus.

Sing, oh, sing, ye chil - dren, Sing ye joy - ful - ly; Christ our Lord hath

ris - en From death's cap - tiv - i - ty. Ris - en is our Sav - iour

Fine.

Christ our Lord and King, Therefore sing ye prais- es, Joy - ful hom-age bring.

1. Dark and sad the evening, When his foes prevail'd, When our Master's Bod - y

To the cross was nailed ; E - vil foes had conquered, Ho - li - ness was

D.C.

slain: Sa - tan then vic - to - rious Ruled the earth a - gain.

[*After last verse repeat Chorus.*]

2 Follow to the garden,
   To the rocky tomb,
Where His friends had laid Him
   In the deepening gloom;
Roman guards are stationed,
   Fixed the Jewish seal,
Lest, by night, the faithful
   Should His Body steal.—*Cho.*

3 Vain were Roman soldiers,
   Vain the Jewish seal,
Christ hath burst the prison!
   Christ hath conquered hell!

Risen is our Saviour!
   Christ our Lord and King!
Therefore sing ye praises,
   Joyful homage bring.—*Cho.*

4 Ever in the heavens
   Reigneth Christ our King,
And, His might extolling,
   We His praises sing;
Sing the wondrous story
   Of the joyful hour,
When the grave was conquered
   By His mighty power.—*Cho.*

89. EASTER CAROL.

Miss Beewster, *Detroit, Mich.*   S. J. Vail. *By permission.*

1. Rise we so joy - ful, make no de - lay, Haste we our ear - ly hom -

age to pay! Bring we sweet in - cense of ca - rol'd praise, This is our

Eas - ter! bright queen of days! This is our Eas- ter! bright queen of days!

Chorus.

Break forth in sing - ing, Shout your loudest praise! Christ is a ris - en,

An - cient of Days! Christ is a - ris - en, An - cient of Days!

2 Jesu, the Saviour, bore cross and shame;
  Christ by His Easter won kingly name!
  Jesu, our Saviour, hallowed the grave;
  Christ has redeemed us, mighty to save!—*Cho.*

3 Jesu, our Saviour, bore grief and pain;
  Christ for us suffered not all in vain!
  Jesu, dear Saviour, lived to obey;
  Christ, the Redeemer, opens Heaven to-day!—*Cho.*

4 Jesu, our Saviour, suffered earth's needs;
  Christ, the Redeemer, now intercedes!
  Jesu, our Saviour, suffered alone;
  Christ is now seated on the White Throne!—*Cho.*

5 After the dark night comes the bright day,
  Clear from death's shadows see Living Way!
  Where is grave's victory? where is death's sting?
  Christ is arisen! Christ is our King!—*Cho.*

92. WHITSUN-DAY ANTHEM.

Ps. lviii. 6, 9, 11.   GILL.

Set up Thy-self, O God,   Set   up   Thy-

Set   up   Thy-self, O   God,   a-
Set   up   Thy-

self,   O   God,

bove the heav'ns, a-bove the heav'ns, and Thy   glo-ry,   Thy
self,   O   God,

Set up Thy-self, O God, a-bove the   heav'ns, and Thy

glo-ry   a-bove   all   the earth.   A-wake up,   my

glo-ry,   a-wake, a-wake, a-wake up, my glo-ry, a-wake, lute and harp; I my - self will a - wake, will a - wake right

harp...............

ear - ly.   For the great-ness of Thy

For the great-ness of Thy mer -

For the great-ness of Thy mer - cy, of Thy

mer - cy reach - eth un - to the heav'ns, and Thy

cy reach - - eth,

mer - cy reach - eth,

truth un - to the clouds, Thy truth un - to the clouds.

93. TRINITY-TIDE ANTHEM.

Ps. xxvii. 4.   MACFARREN.

One thing have I de - sir - ed of the Lord, One thing have I de -

sir - ed of the Lord, af - ter that will I seek, | 1st time. | 2d time. seek; that I may

dwell in the house of the Lord all the days of my life,

to be - hold the beau - ty of the Lord,....... and to in -

quire in His tem - ple; to be - hold the beau - ty of the

Lord,......... and to in - quire.... in His tem - ple.

94. TRINITY-TIDE ANTHEM.

Ps. cxxv. 1.

MACFARREN.

They that put their trust in the Lord,.. They that put their trust in the

Lord... shall be e - ven as the Mount Si - on, shall be

e - ven as the Mount Si - on, which may not be re -

mov - ed, but stand-eth fast for ev - er. A - - men.

95. THERE'S A FRIEND.

1. There's a Friend for lit - tle chil - dren A - bove the bright blue sky,
   A .... Friend that nev - er chan - ges, Whose love will nev - er die;

Un - like our friends by na - ture, Who change with chang-ing years,

This Friend is al - ways wor - thy The precious Name He bears. *A - men.*

2 There's a rest for little children
   Above the bright blue sky,
   Who love the blessed Saviour
   And to His Father cry:
   A rest from every trouble
   From sin and sorrow free:
   There every little pilgrim
   Shall rest eternally.

3 There's a home for little children,
   Above the bright blue sky,
   Where Jesus reigns in glory,
   A home of peace and joy;
   No home on earth is like it,
   Nor can with it compare,
   For every one is happy,
   Nor can be happier there.

4 There's a crown for little children,
   Above the bright blue sky,
   And all who look to Jesus
   Shall wear it by and by:
   A crown of brightest glory
   Which He shall sure bestow,
   On all who love the Saviour,
   And walk with Him below.

5 There's a song for little children,
   Above the bright blue sky,
   And a harp of sweetest music
   For their hymn of victory:
   And all above is pleasure,
   And found in Christ alone;
   O come, dear little children,
   That all may be your own. Amen.

96. ONE THERE IS.

MOZART.

1. One there is a - bove all oth - ers Well deserves the name of Friend;

His is love be - yond a brother's, Cost - ly, free, and knows no end.

Which of all our friends to save us, Could or would have shed his blood ?

But this Sav - iour died to have us Re - con - ciled, in Him, to God.

2 When He lived on earth abased,
　Friend of sinners was His name;
Now, above all glory raised,
　He rejoices in the same.
Oh, for grace our hearts to soften!
　Teach us, Lord, at length to love ;
We, alas! forget too often
　What a Friend we have above. Amen.

97. A THANKSGIVING HYMN.

J. A. P. Schulze.

1. We plow the fer - tile mead - ows, And sow the fur-row'd land, But

yet the wav - ing har - vest De-pends on God's own hand; It is His

mer - cy gives us The sunshine and the rain, That paints in ver - dant

beau - ty The mountain and the plain. Ev - ery bless-ing we en - joy

Comes to us from God; Then praise His name, Then praise His name, For

He is ev - er good, For He is ev - er good.

2 By Him were all things fashioned,
　Around us and afar;
　He made the earth and ocean,
　And every shining star;
　He made the pleasant spring-time,
　The summer bright and warm,
　The golden days of autumn,
　The winter and the storm.—*Cho.*

3 He makes the glorious sun-set,
　The moon to sail on high;
　He bids the breezes fan us,
　And stormy clouds to fly;
　He gives us every blessing;
　To Him our lives we owe;
　He sent His Son to save us
　From sin, and death, and woe.—*Cho.*

98. ART THOU WEARY.

1. Art thou wea - ry, art thou lan - guid, Art thou sore dis - trest?

"Come to me," saith One, "and com - ing, Be at rest."

2 Hath He marks to lead me to Him,
　If He be my guide?
"In His Feet and Hands are Wound-
　And His Side!" [prints,

3 Hath He Diadem as Monarch
　That His Brow adorns?
"Yea, a Crown, in very surety,
　But of thorns."

4 If I find Him, if I follow,
　What His guerdon here?
"Many a sorrow, many a labor,
　Many a tear."

5 If I still hold closely to Him,
　What hath He at last?
"Sorrow vanquished, labor ended,
　Jordan past."

6 If I ask Him to receive me,
　Will He say me nay?
"Not till earth, and not till heaven
　Pass away."

7 Finding, following, keeping, struggling,
　Is He sure to bless?
"Angels, Martyrs, Prophets, Virgins,
　Answer, Yes!"

99. THE LABORERS ARE FEW.

Rev. J. H. W.

1. The fields are all white, And the Rea-pers are few— We children are
2. Our hands are so small, And our works are so weak, We can-not teach

willing, But what can we do, To work for our Lord in His har - vest?
oth-ers—How then shall we seek To work for our Lord in His har - vest?

3 We'll work by our prayers,
   By the pennies we bring,
   By small self-denials—
   The least little thing
May work for our Lord in His harvest.

4 Until, by and by,
   As the years pass, at length
   We too may be Reapers,
   And go forth in strength
To work for our Lord in His harvest.

100. THY WILL BE DONE.

A-men.

1 My God, my Father, | while I | stray,
   Far from my home, in | life's rough | way,
   Oh, teach me from my | heart to | say,
      "Thy | will be | done."

2 Though dark my path, and | sad my | lot,
   Let me be still and | murmur | not,
   Or breathe the prayer di-|vinely | taught,
    . . "Thy | will be | done."

8 What though in lonely | grief I | sigh
   For friends beloved no | longer | nigh,
   Submissive would I | still re- | ply,
      "Thy | will be | done."

4 If Thou shouldst call me | to re- | sign
   What most I prize, it | ne'er was | mine;
   I only yield Thee | what is | Thine;
      "Thy | will be | done."

61. RUSSIAN HYMN.

1. { Sav - iour, breathe an eve-ning bless-ing, Ere re - pose our spi - rits seal;
   Sin and want we come con - fess-ing, Thou canst save, and Thou a - lone, }

Hal - le - lu - jah, Hal - le - lu - jah, Hal - le - lu - jah. A - men.

2. { Tho' destruc - tion walk a-round us, Though the ar - rows past us fly,
   An - gel guards from Thee surround us, We are safe if Thou art nigh. }

Hal - le - lu - jah, Hal - le - lu - jah, Hal - le - lu - jah. A - men.

3 Though the night be dark and dreary,
   Darkness cannot hide from Thee!
Thou our shepherd, never weary,
   Watches where Thy people be. Hallelujah, &c.

4 Should swift death this night o'ertake us,
   And our bed become our tomb,
May the morn in heav'n awake us,
   Clad in bright and deathless bloom. Hallelujah, &c.

INDEX OF FIRST LINES.

www.ingramcontent.com/pod-product-compliance
Lightning Source LLC
Chambersburg PA
CBHW020253290326
41930CB00039B/1178